Material Detectives: Wa...

Let's Look at a Puddle

Angela Royston

First published in Great Britain by Raintree,
Halley Court, Jordan Hill, Oxford OX2 8EJ,
part of Harcourt Education.
Raintree is a registered trademark of Harcourt
Education Ltd.

Editorial: Andrew Farrow and Sarah Chappelow
Design: Jo Malivoire and AMR
Picture Research: Erica Newbery
Production: Duncan Gilbert

Originated by Modern Age
Printed and bound in China by South China
Printing Company

10 digit ISBN 1 844 43635 7 (hardback)
13 digit ISBN 978 1 844 43635 4 (hardback)
10 09 08 07 06
10 9 8 7 6 5 4 3 2 1

10 digit ISBN 1 844 43640 3 (paperback)
13 digit ISBN 978 1 844 43640 8 (paperback)
11 10 09 08 07
10 9 8 7 6 5 4 3 2 1

British Library Cataloguing in Publication Data
Royston, Angela
Water: let's look at a puddle – (Material
Detectives)
620.1'98
A full catalogue record for this book is available
from the British Library

Acknowledgements
The publishers would like to thank the following
for permission to reproduce photographs:
Alamy pp. 22 left, 24 top; Creatas pp. 20, 23
(solid); David Muench/Corbis p. 10; Getty
Images/Photodisc pp. 19, 23 (float); Ivan J
Belcher/Worldwide Picture Library/Alamy pp. 22
right, 24 bottom; Lesley Pardoe/PBPA (Paul Beard
Photo Library) pp. backcover (splash), 18;
National Geographic/Getty pp. 4, 23 (dip);
Photodisc p. 16; Picture Plain/Photolibrary pp.
15, 23 (disappear); Rebecca Emery/Corbis p. 5;
Sarah Chappelow pp. 21, 23 (melts); Satushek
Steve/Photolibrary pp. backcover (rain), 9;
Star/Zefa p. 14; stock4b/Felbert + Eickenberg/zefa
p. 13; Tudor Photography/ Harcourt Education
Ltd pp. 6, 7, 8, 11, 12, 17, 23 (liquid).

Cover photograph of puddles reproduced with
permission of Comstock Images/Getty Images.

Every effort has been made to contact copyright
holders of any material reproduced in this book.
Any omissions will be rectified in subsequent
printings if notice is given to the publishers.

The paper used to print this book comes from
sustainable resources.

Some words are shown in bold, **like this**. You can find them in the glossary on page 23.

Contents

What is a puddle?

A puddle is a small pool of water.

A puddle forms in a **dip** in the ground.

Some puddles are deeper than other puddles.

What is water?

Water is a **liquid**.

Liquids are wet and runny.

water

milk

banana

biscuit

Which of these things are liquids?

Milk and water are **liquids**.

They are both wet and runny.

Water falls from the sky as rain.

It makes puddles on the ground.

What shape are puddles?

Puddles are many different shapes and sizes.

Water runs all over the place.

So puddles can be any shape.

Can puddles change size?

You can make a puddle bigger by pouring more water into it.

What happens to a puddle when the sun shines on it?

A puddle gets smaller when the sun shines on it.

The sun makes the water dry up.

If the sun shines for a long time, a puddle will **disappear**.

How can you make a splash?

When you jump into a puddle, you make a big splash.

stone

brick

leaf

twig

If you threw these things into a big puddle, which ones would make a splash?

The stone and the brick would make a splash because they are heavy.

Some things **float** on water.

The leaf and the twig would float in the puddle.

When does a puddle turn into ice?

A puddle turns into ice when it gets very cold.

Ice is **solid** water.

When the ice **melts**, it turns back into water.

Quiz

Which of these puddles will get bigger?

Which puddle will get smaller?

Look for the answer on page 24.

Glossary

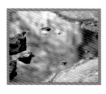
dip
a shallow hole or hollow

disappear
go away so that you cannot see it

float
not sink to the bottom

liquid
something you can pour and is not solid

melts
becomes warmer and turns from a solid into a liquid

solid
something that keeps its shape by itself

Index

Answer to quiz on page 22

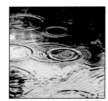 The puddle in the rain is getting bigger because more water is falling into it.

 The puddle in the sun will get smaller because the sun will dry up the water.

Note to parents and teachers

Reading for information is an important part of a child's literacy development. Learning begins with a question about something. Help children think of themselves as investigators and researchers by encouraging their questions about the world around them. Each chapter in this book begins with a question. Read the question together. Look at the pictures. Talk about what you think the answer might be. Then read the text to find out if your predictions were correct. Think of other questions you could ask about the topic, and discuss where you might find the answers. Assist children in using the picture glossary and the index to practice new vocabulary and research skills.